# The Creation and Flood Stories

## An Introductory Aid to Understanding Source and Redaction Criticism

Henry E. Neufeld

EnerPower Press

Gonzalez, FL

2020

EnerPower Press is an imprint of Energion Publications

ISBN: 978-1-63199-525-5

eISBN: 978-1-63199-526-2

EnerPower Press

P. O. Box 841

Gonzalez, FL 32560

energion.com

EnerPower Press is an imprint of Energion Publications

# TABLE OF CONTENTS

Introduction..............................................................................................................1
    FORMAT OF THE TRANSLATION AND NOTES ...........................................1

      Elements Common In Genesis 1:1-2:3 ...........................................................2

The Priestly Creation Story ...................................................................................2
    Overview ............................................................................................................2

    Texts ..................................................................................................................2

          GENESIS 1                                 2

          GENESIS 2                                 3

The Yahwist Story ..................................................................................................4
    Introduction .......................................................................................................4

    Genesis 2 ...........................................................................................................4

    TRANSLATION AND TEXTUAL NOTES .......................................................5

    CONTENT NOTES .............................................................................................5

The Two Flood Stories ...........................................................................................7
    A Comparison of the *J* and *P* Accounts ...............................................................7

    Color Coded Text ............................................................................................12

          GENESIS 6                               13

          GENESIS 7                               13

          CHAPTER 8                              14

Reflections ............................................................................................................15

For Further Study ................................................................................................15

# INTRODUCTION

In studying biblical languages in college and graduate school I frequently encountered use of the various forms of biblical criticism. Over the last few decades, critical disciplines have multiplied, so that there are a variety of tools for the serious Bible student. Rhetorical criticism, for example, has gained wide acceptance and use. The three major tools I encountered, however, were form criticism, source criticism, and redaction criticism. These three deal with the prehistory of the text, while textual criticism deals with transmission after the text has attained a generally stable written form.

Form criticism deals with oral transmission of a text and the impact this has on what comes through in the final document. Source criticism deals with prior documents that become references for, or are included in, the final document. Redaction criticism deals with the way an author or redactor brings these prior elements, along with original contributions, into the text that we study.

The following translation and notes is designed to illustrate some points of source and structure in the Genesis creation stories. It is not intended as a full exposition of the various issues involved, but rather as a tool to help understand them. I discuss issues of the historical-critical method further in the FastTracts booklet *What is Biblical Criticism?* available from Energion Publications, and I discuss the theology of creation and the implications of various types of criticism on our understanding in the book *God the Creator* in the Topical Line Drives Series.

It illustrates primarily source and redaction issues, but it does touch on form criticism as we look at potential interpolations, and also on rhetorical criticism as we look at the way the text is structured to present a particular message.

The translation is mine, and I have done some things to try to clarify the structure even though this often results in a less natural translation in English. I do not recommend my translation for reading comfort, but I believe it does well in helping to answer the questions often posed about this text:

- What is the primary intention of the author(s)?
- Is this a single story or multiple stories?
- Is there scientific evidence available from this text?
- What cosmological assumptions are involved?

Obviously I will not answer all these questions in a single translation with notes. What I hope is that this translation will help others answer those questions for themselves.

## FORMAT OF THE TRANSLATION AND NOTES

There are three sources in the text of this translation. The font, size, and style of text remains in accordance with the source. The color and background reflect structural elements as designated below. The source fonts are:

- Interpolations
  Text that is from none of the major sources

- Text from the priestly source
  Priestly Source, commonly designated *P*

- Text from the Yahwist source
  Yahwist (Jahwist) source, commonly designated *J*

The following text colors are used to highlight particular phraseology illustrating theme and structure.

**ELEMENTS COMMON IN GENESIS 1:1-2:3**

1. God created/made
2. God said
3. Let there be
4. It was so
5. God called/named
6. God saw that it was good
7. There was evening and there was morning
8. the _____ day
9. Divided

**ADDITIONAL ELEMENT COMMON IN GENESIS 2:4FF**

10. Personal actions of God—formed, planted and so forth
11. God created/made

Verse numbers are indicated by superscripted numbers ([1]). Notes on the translation and text are indicated by lower case letters in square brackets [a] with links to the note included. Notes on the content are indicated by numbers in square brackets [1].

# THE PRIESTLY CREATION STORY

## OVERVIEW

Often people refer to the Genesis creation stories as myths, but this is not technically correct in reference to Genesis 1. The priestly account is liturgy. It justifies and underlies the celebration of a worship cycle of seven days. If you look at the color coding below you will see how much of the text consists of formal elements that tend to outline and drive the text. This is carefully written theology.

Besides its liturgical purpose (as liturgy and justifying liturgy) it is tightly written theology. Elements of this story explicitly contradict the Mesopotamian stories. Where there is conflict in the Mesopotamian accounts, there is no conflict here. Where there is expressed concern about the outcome there, there is none here. The key focus of the structure and vocabulary is to express the simple, uncontested power of God exercised in forming the world as we know it.

At the same time as it contradicts elements of the Mesopotamian stories, it also is founded in a similar cosmology. This cosmology has the world as a fixed area of land, above and surrounded (horizontally) by a primeval ocean, and a dome (sky or firmament) stretched above that. Water exists above the firmament as well.

## TEXTS

### Genesis 1

[1] In the beginning [a] God created heaven and earth.

[2] Now the earth was [b] formless and empty, and there was darkness above primeval ocean, [1] and God's wind [2][c] was blowing above the water. [3] Then God said, "Let there be light, and there was light.» [4] And God saw that the light was good, and God divided the light from the darkness. [5] And God called the light day, and he

called the darkness night. So there was evening, and there was morning, day one.

[6] Then God said, "Let there be a dome [4] between the waters, and let it divide between water and water." [7] And God made the dome, and he divided the water that was under the dome from the water that was above the dome, and it was so. [8] And God called the dome heaven, and there was evening and there was morning, a second day.

[9] Then God said, "Let the waters under heaven be gathered to one place, and let the dry land be visible." And it was so. [10] And God called the dry land earth, and the gathering of the water he called seas, and God saw that it was good. [11] And God said, "Let the earth produce vegetation, herbs bearing seed and fruit trees bearing fruit with the seed in it according to its kind upon the earth, and it was so. [12] And the earth produced vegetation, herbs bearing seed according to its kind and trees bearing fruit whose seed is in it according to their kind. And God saw that it was good. [13] And there was evening and there was morning, a third day.

[14] Then God said, "Let there be lights in the dome of heaven to divide the day from the night, and let them be for signs and for appointed times, and for days and years. [15] And let them be for lights in the dome of heaven to give light on the earth.» And it was so. [16] So God made two great lights, the big light to rule the day and the little light to rule the night, and also the stars. [17] And God placed them in the dome of heaven to give light on the earth, [18] and to rule the day and the night and to divide the light from the darkness. And God saw that it was good. [19] And there was evening and there was morning, a fourth day.

[20] And God said, "Let the water swarm with swarming creatures that are alive, and let birds fly above the earth on the face of the dome of heaven. [21] So God created great sea serpents, and every living creature that moves that the water brought forth according to its kind and every flying bird according to its kind. And God saw that it was good. [22] And God blessed them, saying, «Bring forth fruit and multiply, and fill the water in the seas, and let birds multiply in the earth.» [23] And there was evening and there was morning, a fifth day.

[24] And God said, "Let the earth bring forth living creatures according to their kind, domestic animals and creatures that move, and land animals according to their kinds.» And it was so. [25] And God made the land animals according to their kinds, and the domestic animals according to their kinds, and every moving land creature according to its kind. And God saw that it was good. [26] Then God said, "Let us make humanity [3] in our form,[4] according to our appearance, and let them rule over the fish of the sea and the birds of heaven and the cattle and over all the earth, and over all the moving creatures that move on the earth. [27] And God created humanity in his form. He created it [e] in the form of God. He created them male and female. [28] And God blessed them and God said to them, «Bring forth fruit and multiply and fill the earth and bring it into subjection and rule over the fish of the sea and over the birds of heaven and over every living creature that moves on the earth. [29] And God said, "Look! I've given you every herb giving seed which is on all the earth and every tree which has on it the fruit of a seed bearing tree. They will be yours to eat. [30] And to every beast of the earth and to every bird of heaven and to every moving creation on the earth which has in it a living soul will belong every green plant for food. And it was so. [31] And God saw everything he had made, and yes, it was very good. And there was evening and there was morning, a sixth day.

## Genesis 2

[1] And heaven and earth were finished and all their host. [2] And on the seventh day God put and end to his work that he had done, and he rested on the seventh day from all his work that he had done. [3] And God blessed the seventh day, and set it apart, because in it he rested from all his work that God did in creating.

# THE YAHWIST STORY

## INTRODUCTION

This story looks at creation from a completely different angle. Here God is personally and actively involved in the creation process and is visible to the newly created human for whom he seeks a helper. Rather than simple commands which are fulfilled, there is formation and growth. The chronology is also not precisely the same. It is unlikely that an editor heavily concerned with chronology would have put these stories together. On the other hand, someone more concerned with theology could easily see these two aspects of God's power–creative force and personal attention–as being complementary and presenting a more complete image of God. I argue elsewhere that Psalm 104 is another creation story with the focus there being on the continuing creative and sustaining power rather than the initiation.

4These are the records of heaven and earth when they were created, in the day when YHWH [5] [d] God made earth and heaven,5 and every shrub of the field before it was on the earth, and every green plant of the field before it sprouted, because YHWH God had not caused it to rain on the earth, and there was no human being to till the ground. 6 And a stream used to go up from the earth and it watered all the face of the ground.

## GENESIS 2

7 And YHWH God formed a human being from dust from the ground, and breathed into its [e] nostrils living breath, and the human became a living creature. 8 And YHWH God planted a garden in Eden, to the east, and there he placed the human being whom he had formed.

9 And YHWH God made every tree that was nice to look at and good for food sprout from the ground, and the tree of life in the middle of the garden, and the tree of the knowledge of good and evil.

10 And a river went out from Eden to water the garden and from there it separated and became four heads. 11 The name of the one was Pishon. It is the one that surrounds the whole land of Havilah where there is gold. 12 And the gold from that land is good, there are bdellium and onyx stones. 13 And the name of the second river is Gihon. It is the one that goes around the whole land of Cush. 14 And the name of the third river was Hideqel. It's the one that goes to the east of Ashur, and the fourth river is Perath (Euphrates). [6]

15 And YHWH God took the human and placed it [e] in the garden of Eden to cultivate it and to guard it. 16 And YHWH God commanded the human saying, «From all the trees of the garden you may certainly eat, 17 but from the tree of knowledge of good and evil you may not eat from it, because in the day you eat from it you will definitely die.

18 And YHWH God said, "It is not good for the human to be alone. I will make for it a suitable helper.» 19 So YHWH God formed [6] from the ground every beast of the field and every bird of heaven, and he brought them to the human to see what he would call them. And whatever the human called a living thing, that was its name. 20 And the human gave names to all the beasts, and to the birds of the heavens, and to all the beasts of the field, but for the human there was not found a suitable helper. 21 And YHWH God made the human sleep deeply, so it slept and God took one of its ribs and closed the flesh instead of it. 22 And YHWH God made the rib which he had taken from the human into a woman, and he brought her to the human. 23And the human said, "This now is bone of my bones and flesh from my flesh. She will be called woman (ishshah) because she was taken from

man (ish)." [24] For this reason a man will leave his father and his mother and will cleave to his wife, and they will become one flesh. [25] And the two of them were both naked, the human and his wife, and they were not ashamed.

## TRANSLATION AND TEXTUAL NOTES

a.  The first word of the Bible is a textual problem. A considerable difference in translation would result from different pointing or from some different possible translations of the first two words. The major options are "In the beginning God created" or "When God began creating." I choose the former, but I recognize that there is a considerable basis for the alternative.

b.  The ruin and restoration theory requires the translation "became" here, since this theory holds that the earth was created, as described in Genesis 1:1, and then destroyed (and the earth *became* formless and empty) and then was created again as described in verses 2 and following. This is, however, an extremely improbable translation of the passage. Frequently, the verb «hayah» is used in the perfect following the subject simply meaning "to be" rather than "become" or "happen" as it does in most passages when it precedes the subject. Another option is the pluperfect meaning, "the earth had been". In either case, this is not a story about creation from nothing, but rather of formation out of chaos which is already presented as existing.

c.  I translate "God's Wind" rather than "God's Spirit" because of the parallels and because it is blowing over or above the waters.

d.  I use YHWH for the proper name of God in order to let readers know where it is used, and to allow them to choose whether and how to pronounce it.

e.  With a certain amount of concern about the impression I will cause, I use "it" to refer to the human being as first created before we have the identification of the genders at the end of the chapter. Even though *'adam* is grammatically masculine, it refers to the person as a human being, and not specifically to gender, which is made clear later. Thus I use "it" in English (Hebrew does not have a neuter) to help produce the same suspense that the original does. Be aware that all pronouns in Hebrew referring to the first human are masculine.

## CONTENT NOTES

1.  *Tehom*, or the primeval ocean is what there is before the creation. We will see this again in the flood as the fountains are opened up from the *tehom* as part of the flood. This is linguistically related to the Mesopotamian *Tiamat* though here it does not have personality and takes no action as it does in the Mesopotamian tales. It is completely subject to God's action.

2.  Again we have an element that compares to the Mesopotamian stories, but again its function is different. God's wind seems positively inactive, whereas in the Babylonian story it is Marduk's primary weapon.

3.  I use either "humanity" or "human" throughout to translate the Hebrew *'adam*, thus distinguishing it from *'iysh* or «man (a male person)». The latter term is not introduced until the end of chapter 2.

4.  It is hard to find a translation here that would truly be neutral in English. Whether this is a moral and ethical form or pattern, or whether it was intended as a physical form is a matter for interpretation.

5.  One literary characteristic that changes between the two stories is the name for God, with the more generic *'elohim* used in Genesis 1:1-2:3, but the proper name along with the generic title used in 2:4ff.

6.  This is identified as an interpolation because it disrupts both the subject matter and the syntactical flow of the chapter. Amongst other things there is a long sequence of verbs that begins in verse five and continues through most of the chapter. The editor probably placed it here to relate it to the stream identified in verse 6.

7.  In trying to solve the differences in chronology between the two creation stories many read "had formed" here (pluperfect). It is possible for the form to be translated that way, but not likely. Normally, the pluperfect is indicated by a switch to the perfect in a sequence of imperfects with the waw-consecutive as are shown here. In addition, the story flows perfectly as it is. Be wary of forcing the text into a mold.

# THE TWO FLOOD STORIES

## A COMPARISON OF THE *J* AND *P* ACCOUNTS

Many Bible readers have some difficulty understanding the point of the source theories about the Pentateuch, and what the resulting source documents would have been like. It is not my intent in this document to fully explain or defend the source theory, but rather to provide an example of an instance of disentangling two sources according to the source theory, and to make it easy to see what the individual hypothetical source stories would have looked like.

Readers should be aware that all dating of sources is very tentative. It's hard enough to date a complete piece of literature, but when one is instead dating the remains of one as they show up in a later, edited work, the task can be overwhelming. In this 9/11/06 revision, I'm including some additional dating options for the various sources.

Source theory in the Pentateuch is often referred to by the abbreviation **JEPD,** which comes from the initials for the four hypothetical sources:

J  Yahwist (Jahvist), named for characteristic use of the name YHWH, though this is only one of many characteristics. Usually dated in the 11th-10th centuries BCE.

Elohist, named for characteristic use of the name "Elohim" for God. Usually dated in the 8thcentury BCE.

E  Note that while the source is named for the usage of a particular name for God, that is not the only distinguishing characteristic. One can't simply go to Genesis, pick out any passage that uses "Elohim" and assume it's from the Elohist. At a minimum, one might include many priestly passages by that means.

Priestly Source, named for its concern with the temple and its rituals. Usually dated around the time of the exile in the 6th century BCE.

P  The post-exilic dating for the priestly source should be challenged, and has been. Jacob Milgrom suggests that most of the Pentateuch, except for a few minor interpolations, was completed prior to the exile. (See Milgrom, Anchor Bible: Leviticus, Volume 1, pp. 3-35.) Many modern commentaries also divide the priestly source into multiple strata, with a minimum of a separate H (holiness) and P source. These strata to not impact the passage in question here.

Deuteronomist, named for Deuteronomy which is largely from this source, and dated by many to the reform of Josiah in 622 BCE.

D  Again, many date this source much earlier, and I tend to agree that it might date back from as early as Hezekiah's reform. The reason is that I think it would be easier to discover a work that had existed for some time than to invent one and pretend it had just been discovered. In addition, much of Hezekiah's reform seems related to the work of the Deuteronomist. Again, however, this material does not impact the passage under consideration here.

While JEPD is not a terribly accurate abbreviation, since there are more sources in the Pentateuch than those four, and since not all four appear over large sections, it is still convenient shorthand.

The division of the two accounts is that of Gerhard von Rad in his commentary on Genesis. I have chosen to do my own translation and notes for this comparison. The first column is the J account, the second is notes, the third is the P account. The flood account only contains material from two of the four hypothetical sources. To help clarify the differences in the stories, I have rendered Yahweh, or YHWH as 'YHWH' and Elohim as Elohim rather than by their traditional English translations of 'LORD' and 'God.'

The purpose of this document is to provide persons who are not well acquainted with the Biblical languages or source and redaction criticism with a convenient way to see how this method works in a common passage of scripture. The translations are designed to make each story look coherent in itself as much as possible. To compare these to a standard translation, I would recommend reading them in the New Revised Standard Version. See below for additional source information.

## SEPARATED TEXT

The following section presents the text divided into two stories.

The left hand column is the story according to the Yahwist, the center is my notes on that section of the story, and the third is the priestly account. Note that in combining the two sources into a single story (known technically as redaction), the redactor may have used only selected portions of his source, so that we do not have the full story in a single source.

The ideal way to study this is to read the first column through and then think about what the story portrays with just those words. Then do the same thing to the third column. Only after you have gotten a clear idea in your mind of each story should you look at the notes in the center column and reflect on both. To do this is to study what may be the sources of the text as we have it in Genesis.

Finally, go to a standard Bible translation, such as the New Revised Standard Version, and read chapters 6-9. Is the impression of the story different? This last assignment is to try to think like a redaction critic by looking at what the person who brought the text together as it is might have intended.

## J (The Yahwist)

⁵And YHWH saw that the evil of humanity was great on the land, and the whole thrust of his thoughts was only evil continually. ⁶And YHWH was sorry that he had made humanity on the land, and it made him sad in his heart. ⁷And YHWH said, "I will wipe humanity which I created from the face of the ground, from human beings to cattle, to creeping things, to the birds of the heavens, because I'm sorry that I made them!" ⁸But Noah found favor in the eyes of YHWH.

## Notes

*J* has no equivalent of the many instructions in this prologue which includes the genealogy of Noah, the instructions for the ark, and the instructions on creatures to bring into the ark. Some scholars would debate the inclusion of the phrase "These are the generations of Noah" as part of the *P* account, and would instead postulate that it comes from an additional genealogies source. Others would see that source standing behind *P*.

The *J* introduction is shorter, but also has some theology, which would certainly disturb many modern readers.

## P (The Priestly Account)

⁹These are the generations of Noah. Noah was a righteous man, who was perfect in his generation. Noah walked with Elohim. ¹⁰And Noah fathered three sons: Shem, Ham and Japheth. ¹¹Now the earth became corrupt before Elohim, and it was filled with violence. ¹²And Elohim saw that the earth was corrupt, because all flesh had corrupted its behavior upon the earth.

¹³And Elohim said to Noah: "The end of all flesh has come before me, because the land is filled with violence because of them, so I'm going to wipe them off the earth. ¹⁴Make for yourself an ark of gofer wood, with rooms shall you make it, and cover it inside and out with pitch. ¹⁵You are to make it this way: The ark will be 300 cubits long and 50 cubits wide and 30 cubits high. ¹⁶You will make a roof for the ark and complete it a cubit above, and you shall make a door of the ark in its side. Make it with a lower, second and third deck. ¹⁷And as for me, I am bringing the flood of water upon the land to destroy all flesh that has in it a living spirit under the whole heavens. Everything that is on the earth shall die.

¹⁸And I will raise up my covenant with you, and you will enter the ark, you and your sons and your wife, and your sons' wives.

[1]Then YHWH said to Noah, "Go, you and all your household into the ark, because you I have seen righteous before me in this generation. [2]From all the clean beasts take seven pairs, each with its mate, and from the beasts which are not clean take two, each with its mate. [3]Also from the birds of heaven, seven pairs, male and female, so there will be seed on the face of all the land.[4]Because in seven days I will make it rain upon the earth for forty days and forty nights, and I will wipe out all that lives that I have made from upon the face of the ground." [5]And Noah did all that YHWH commanded him.

{7:7}So Noah, his sons, his wife and his son's wives went to the ark, from the face of the flood, {7:16b} and YHWH shut him in.

[8]From the clean beasts and from the beasts which were not clean and from the birds and from everything that creeps on the ground [9]two went in to Noah into the ark, male and female as Elohim commanded Noah.

Note that in the **P** account, there is detailed information about the chronology of the flood, but the seven day warning is not mentioned. In **J**, on the other hand, the information is very brief.

The J account refers only to rain, and not to the fountains of the Tehom or the windows of the heavens.

Note the single instance of "Elohim" in the **J** text.

[19]And from all life, from all flesh, you shall bring two from all of them into the ark, to let them live with you. They shall be male and female. [20]From the birds according to their kinds and from the cattle according to their kinds, from all things that creep on the ground according to their kinds, two from every kind shall come to you so they may live. [21]And as for you, take for yourself from all the food which is eaten, and gather it to you and it will be for you and for them to eat. [22]And Noah did according to all that Elohim commanded him.

[6]Now Noah was 600 years old when the flood of water was upon the earth. [11]In the 600th year of the life of Noah, in the second month, in the 17th day of the month, in that day the fountains of the great Tehom were split and the windows of heaven were opened. [13]In that very day Noah, and with him Shem, Ham and Japheth (sons of Noah), and Noah's wife, and his three sons' wives, went into the ark. [14]They and every living creature according to its kind and all the cattle according to their kinds, and all the creeping things that creep on the earth according to their kinds, and all the birds according to their kind, each bird and each winged creature. [15]And they came to Noah into the ark, two by two from all flesh which had in it a living spirit. [16]And those who came in were male and female from all flesh, as Elohim commanded Noah.

{7:10} And the rain was upon the land forty days and forty nights, [17b] and the waters surged up and carried the ark, and the ark rose above the land.

[17]And the flood was upon the land for 40 days. [18]And the waters became great, and grew very, very much on the earth, and the ark was carried along on the waters. [19]And the waters increased very greatly on the land, and the covered all the high mountains which were under all the heavens. [20]The waters rose till they were 15 cubits above the mountain tops.

[22]Everything that had living breath in its nostrils, from all which was on the dry land perished. [23]So he [YHWH] wiped out every living thing which was on the face of the ground, from man to beast to creeping thing to the birds of the heavens, and they were wiped out from the land. Only Noah and those who were with him remained.

[21]And all flesh that creeps on the earth, and birds, and cattle, and living creatures and from all swarming creatures that swarm on the land, and all the people died. [24]And the waters rose greatly against the land for 150 days.

{8:6a} At the end of forty days {8:2b} the rain ceased from the heavens. {8:3a} And the waters went away steadily from upon the land {8:6b} and Noah opened a window of the ark that he had made.

There is again no detailed chronology and no reference to the length of time the waters were over the earth in the *J* account, while the *P* account covers this in great detail.

[1]And Elohim remembered Noah, and all the living creatures, and all the cattle which were with him in the ark, and Elohim made a wind to pass over the earth, and the waters receded. [2]And the fountains of the Tehom and the windows of heaven were closed. [3b]After 150 days the waters had receded. [4]And the ark rested in the seventh month on the seventeenth day of the month on the mountains of Ararat. [5]The waters were going and receding until the 10th month; in the 10th month, on the 1st day of the month, when the tops of the mountains were seen.

⁸Then Noah sent forth the dove from him to see if the waters had ceased from upon the face of the ground. ⁹But the dove could not find rest for her feet, and she returned to him at the ark, because the waters were upon the face of the whole land. And he reached out his hand and took her, and brought her unto him in the ark. ¹⁰And he tried again seven days later, and he again sent forth the dove from the ark.¹¹And the dove returned to him at the time of evening, and behold, an olive branch torn off was in her mouth, and Noah knew that the waters had ceased from upon the land. ¹²And He tried again seven days later, and he sent forth the dove, and she no longer returned to the ark.

And Noah put aside the covering of the ark, and he saw, and behold the face of the ground was dry.

²⁰Then Noah built an altar to YHWH, and he took from all the clean beasts and from all the clean birds, and offered burnt offerings on the altar.

²¹And when YWHW smelled the pleasing odor, he said to himself, "I will not again curse the ground because of human beings, because the inclination of a human being's mind is bad from youth, so I will never again smite all living things as I have done. ²²
While there are still days on earth
Planting and harvesting,
Cold and heat,
Summer and winter,
Day and night,
Will not stop.

Contrast the *P* description of sending out a raven until the waters dried up with the specific stories about the dove in *J*.

The priestly source doesn't really conclude until chapter 9. Here it just leaves us with Noah, his families, and all the animals leaving. J concludes with a simple scene of sacrifice.

¹⁵And God spoke to Noah, saying, ¹⁶"Leave the ark, you, your wife, your sons, and your daughters-in-law. ¹⁷Bring out with you all the living creatures from among the birds and the beasts, and from all the crawling things that crawl on the ground, and let them swarm out across the land and be fruitful and multiply on the land. ¹⁸So Noah left, along with his sons, his wife, and his daughters-in-law.¹⁹Every living creature, every crawling thing, every bird, everything that moves about on the land according to their families left the ark.

## COLOR CODED TEXT

The following section presents the text in its canonical form color coded for sources. The sources are Yahwist, Elohist, and interpolation or redactional element.

## Genesis 6

[1]Now when human beings began to get numerous all over the land, and they gave birth to daughters, [2]the sons of God {or "sons of the gods" or "divine beings} saw the daughters of the human beings. They saw that they were good looking, and they took wives for themselves from whomever they chose. [3]Then YHWH said, "My spirit will not always work among human beings, considering that they are flesh. Their lifespan will be 120 years." [4]There were giants {Nephilim} on the earth in those days, and also after the sons of God went to the daughters of the human beings and bore children by them. These were heroes, the famous men of ancient times.

[5]And YHWH saw that the evil of humanity was great on the land, and the whole thrust of human thought was only evil continually. [6]And YHWH was sorry that he had made humanity on the land, and it made him sad in his heart. [7]And YHWH said, "I will wipe humanity which I created from the face of the ground, from human beings to cattle, to creeping things, to the birds in the sky, because I'm sorry that I made them!" [8]But Noah found favor in the eyes of YHWH.

[9]These are the generations of Noah. Noah was a righteous man, who was perfect in his generation. Noah walked with God. [10]And Noah fathered three sons: Shem, Ham and Japheth. [11]Now the earth became corrupt before God, and it was filled with violence. [12]And God saw that the earth was corrupt, because all flesh had corrupted its behavior upon the earth.

[13]And God said to Noah: "The end of all flesh has come before me, because the land is filled with violence because of them, so I'm going to wipe them off the earth. [14]Make for yourself an ark of gofer wood, with rooms shall you make it, and cover it inside and out with pitch. [15]You are to make it this way: The ark will be 300 cubits long and 50 cubits wide and 30 cubits high. [16]You will make a roof for the ark and complete it a cubit above, and you shall make a door of the ark in its side. Make it with a lower, second and third deck. [17]And as for me, I am bringing the flood of water upon the land to destroy all flesh that has in it a living spirit under the whole heavens. Everything that is on the earth shall die.

[18]And I will raise up my covenant with you, and you will enter the ark, you and your sons and your wife, and your sons' wives.

[19]And from all life, from all flesh, you shall bring two from all of them into the ark, to let them survive with you. They shall be male and female. [20]From the birds according to their kinds and from the cattle according to their kinds, from all things that creep on the ground according to their kinds, two from every kind shall come to you so they may survive. [21]And as for you, take for yourself from all the food which is eaten, and gather it to you and it will be for you and for them to eat. [22]And Noah did according to all that God commanded him.

## Genesis 7

[1]Then YHWH said to Noah, "Go, you and all your household into the ark, because you I have seen righteous before me in this generation. [2]From all the clean beasts take seven pairs, each with its mate, and from the beasts which are not clean take two, each with its mate. [3]Also from the birds of heaven, seven pairs, male and female, so there will be seed on the face of all the land. [4]Because in seven days I will make it rain upon the earth for forty days and forty nights, and I will wipe out all that lives that I have made from upon the face of the ground." [5]And Noah did all that YHWH commanded him.

6Now Noah was 600 years old when the flood of water was upon the earth. 7So Noah, his sons, his wife and his son's wives went to the ark, from the face of the flood. 8From the clean beasts and from the beasts which were not clean and from the birds and from everything that creeps on the ground 9two went in to Noah into the ark, male and female as God commanded Noah. 10And after seven days, the waters came upon the land. 11In the 600th year of the life of Noah, in the second month, in the 17th day of the month, in that day the fountains of the great Tehom were split and the windows of heaven were opened. 12And the rain was upon the land forty days and forty nights. 13In that very day Noah, and with him Shem, Ham and Japheth (sons of Noah), and Noah's wife, and his three daughters-in-law, went into the ark. 14They and every living creature according to its kind and all the cattle according to their kinds, and all the creeping things that creep on the earth according to their kinds, and all the birds according to their kind, each bird and each winged creature. 15And they came to Noah into the ark, two by two from all flesh which had in it a living spirit. 16And those who came in were male and female from all flesh, as God commanded Noah. And YHWH closed it up after him. 17And the flood was upon the land for 40 days, and the waters surged up and carried the ark, and the ark rose above the land. 18And the waters became great, and grew very, very much on the earth, and the ark was carried along on the waters. 19And the waters increased very greatly on the land, and they covered all the high mountains which were under all the heavens. 20The waters rose till they were 15 cubits above the mountain tops. 21And all flesh that creeps on the earth, and birds, and cattle, and living creatures and from all swarming creatures that swarm on the land, and all the people died. 22Everything that had living breath in its nostrils, from all which was on the dry land perished. 23So he [YHWH] wiped out every living thing which was on the face of the ground, from man to beast to creeping thing to the birds of the heavens, and they were wiped out from the land. Only Noah and those who were with him remained. 24And the waters rose greatly against the land for 150 days.

## Chapter 8

1And Elohim remembered Noah, and all the living creatures, and all the cattle which were with him in the ark, and Elohim made a wind to pass over the earth, and the waters receded. 2And the fountains of the Tehom and the windows of heaven were closed and the rain ceased from the heavens. 3And the waters went away steadily from upon the land and Noah opened a window of the ark that he had made. After 150 days the waters had receded. 4And the ark rested in the seventh month on the seventeenth day of the month on the mountains of Ararat. 5The waters were going and receding until the 10th month; in the 10th month, on the 1st day of the month, when the tops of the mountains were seen. 6At the end of forty days, Noah opened a window of the ark that he had made. 7and he sent forth a
raven, and it went forth to and fro, until the waters were dried up
from off the earth. 8Then Noah sent forth the dove from him to see if the waters had ceased from upon the face of the ground.

9But the dove could not find rest for her feet, and she returned to him at the ark, because the waters were upon the face of the whole land. And he reached out his hand and took her, and brought her unto him in the ark. 10And he tried again seven days later, and he again sent forth the dove from the ark. 11And the dove returned to him at the time of evening, and behold, an olive branch torn off was in her mouth, and Noah knew that the waters had ceased from upon the land. 12And He tried again seven days later, and he sent forth the dove, and she no longer returned to the ark. 13And in the 601st year, at the beginning, on the first day of the month, the waters were dried up from upon the land. So Noah put aside the covering of the ark, and he saw, and behold the face of the ground was dry. ¹⁴And on the seventeenth day of the second month the land was dry. ¹⁵And God spoke to Noah, saying, ¹⁶"Leave the ark, you, your wife, your sons, and your daughters-in-law. ¹⁷Bring out with you all the living creatures from among the birds and the beasts, and from all the crawling things that crawl on the ground, and let them swarm out across the land and be fruitful and multiply on the land. ¹⁸So Noah left, along with his sons, his wife, and his daughters-in-law. ¹⁹Every living creature, every crawling thing, every bird, everything that moves about on the land according to their families left the ark. ²⁰Then Noah built an altar to YHWH, and he took from all the clean beasts and from all the clean birds, and offered burnt offerings on the altar.

²¹And when YWHW smelled the pleasing odor, he said to himself, "I will not again curse the ground because of human beings, because the inclination of a human being's mind is bad from youth, so I will never again smite all living things as I have done.
²² While there are still days on earth

Planting and harvesting,
Cold and heat,
Summer and winter,
Day and night,
Will not stop.

# REFLECTIONS

This presentation is very brief, but it includes material from some of the most contentious passages in scripture. Various views on origins depend both on how we read the text as we have it, and on how this text came into being.

What I think should be clear, however, is that the basic textual material is much more complex than people often assume, and that it merits much more serious study. What biblical criticism can offer us is a multi-dimensional view of the text. We don't just see what it meant in its final form. We also get to see how it developed, and how the text grew along with the people who used it as sacred material, first oral, then written, and slowly taking shape.

There are a number of resources in the bibliography to help you follow up on this further, but for a study of how inspiration and authority work in a people group or religious movement, let me recommend first Edward W. H. Vick's work *From Inspiration to Understanding*. For a discussion of the varied perspectives on creation found in scripture, see Herold Weiss's book *Creation in Scripture*, also in the bibliography

# FOR FURTHER STUDY

Achtemeier, Paul J. ed. *HarperCollins Bible Dictionary*. San Francisco: Harper Collins Publishers, 1996. ISBN: 0060600373. See especially the article "Sources of the Pentateuch."

Alexander, David ed. *Eerdman's Handbook to the Bible*. Grand Rapids: William B. Eerdmans Publishing Company, 1973. ISBN: 0802806392. See the notes on Genesis 6-9 and the introduction to the Pentateuch, pp. 122-126. Metzger, Bruce M. ed. *The New Oxford Annotated Bible with the Apocryphal/Deuterocanonical Books*. New York: Oxford University Press, 1994. ISBN: 0195283562. See in particularly the introduction to the Pentateuch (XXXV and XXXVI) and the notes on the flood story in Genesis 6-9.

Neufeld, Henry E. ed. *What Is Biblical Criticism?* Gonzalez, Florida: Energion Publications, 2020.

_____. *God the Creator*. Gonzalez, Florida: Energion Publications, 2020.

_____. *When People Speak for God*. Gonzalez, Florida: Energion Publications, 2007.

Noth, Martin. *A History of Pentateuchal Traditions*. Scholars Press, 2000. Originally published in German in 1948.

Perrin, Norman. *What Is Redaction Criticism?* Eugene, Oregon: Wipf and Stock, 2002.

Suggs, M. Jack ed. *The Oxford Study Bible, Revised English Bible with the Apocrypha*. New York: Oxford University Press, 1992. ISBN: 0195290003. See in particularly the introduction to the Pentateuch (pp. 7-9), the notes on the flood story in Genesis 6-9 and the introductory article "Literature of the Ancient Near East" pp. 57-67.

Thompson, Alden. *Inspiration: Hard Questions, Honest Answers*. 2nd Revised Edition. Gonzalez, Florida: Energion Publications, 2016.

Vick, Edward W. H. From Inspiration to Understanding. Gonzalez, Florida: Energion Publications, 2011.

von Rad, Gerhard. *Genesis, Revised Edition*. Philadelphia: The Westminster Press, 1972. ISBN: 0664209572.

Weiss, Herold. *Creation in Scripture*. Gonzalez, Florida: Energion Publications, 2012.